MW00466967

Forgiveness is Bliss

Forgiveness is Bliss

A real life approach to sustained happiness

PATSY J. CANNON

Blissfully Yours Publishing
© Copyright 2012 **Patsy J. Cannon**

Forgiveness Is Bliss
By Patsy J. Cannon

Copyright 2012 © by Patsy J. Cannon. All Rights Reserved. No part, or any portions of this book may be reproduced in any form whatsoever, except in the case of brief quotations used in articles and reviews.

Quotes from *A Course in Miracles* are public domain and is not copy-righted by the author.

ISBN: 978-0-9764031-6-6
First Printing May 2012
Printed in the United States of America

Edited by DeBora M. Ricks
Cover design by Carolyn Sheltraw

For more information:
www.BlissfulLivingCoach.com
peajae151@gmail.com

Like us on FB @ www.Facebook.com/LivingInBliss

*You who want peace
can find it only
by complete forgiveness.*

- A Course in Miracles

To Jaslyn, Jay, Haven and Jonathan,
you make my life grand!

Acknowledgements

Kami, Mikeela, Mikal and Seth, I'm grateful that you chose me to be your mother. And I'm grateful that I gave you so much fodder to one day write your own books. My life would be incomplete without you.

A very special "thank you" to my editor, DeBora M. Ricks, who kept me on track when I doubted my purpose and myself. Yes, the world does need my version of the chocolate chip cookie! And to my wonderful cohorts at Spiritual Empowerment Center in Baltimore, who kept me at my word to finish this endeavor. *The Power of Your Word* took on a whole new meaning for me.

Mr. T, 'thank you.' I am so grateful that you understood the mission. I love you! And to all the souls who have forgiven me and given me a reason to forgive, I thank you. In forgiving you, I have learned to forgive myself.

I am forever grateful to the Holy Spirit! Thank you for always being there, and thank you for making your presence known. What a blessing!

Contents

Introduction

My happiness is my greatest gift to others!
~ This Is Bliss.

I simply chose to forgive because I'm selfish. Yep, you heard me. I forgive because I have come to realize, quite by accident, I must add, that all this forgiveness work made me look younger and feel better. I even became prettier. Check out my before and after photos, and I believe you will agree. As a matter of fact, look at the photos of me with my daughters. They don't look older than their 35 and 30 year old selves respectfully. It's just that I look amazingly young at 56 years old. And I attribute it all to forgiveness.

While I, like many others, gave lip service to the notion that forgiveness is not for the other person, but for me, I knew that I didn't always practice what I espoused. It somehow felt better to hold onto my anger and not forgive. I truly felt that I had every right to be indignant. I didn't just read about Jim Crow, I actually lived it.

I am a dark skinned female who grew up in a "color struck" southern city. I remember quite vividly wanting to get on the swings but being denied the opportunity because I was "Colored." I was four years old. I was a pioneer in integrating my junior high school. The racism that I endured at the time was far too painful for me to bear. I ended up withdrawing, so I didn't complete a full year of school. Teachers, friends and even Sunday school teachers would often isolate darker complexion girls, and boys seemed to always be drawn to lighter skinned females.

Very close family members were molested as children. My mother knew how to discipline only one way—with the STRAP! I didn't get spankings; I got BEATINGS. So if anyone has a right to be angry, it certainly is me.

Fortunately, even at a young age I had some ideas about this thing called forgiveness. Reflecting back, it appears that I somewhat understood the principles of forgiveness. However, I had no idea how to practice them and totally incorporate them into my life. But one thing I did know how to do was to forget! I realized early on that I would conveniently forget a lot of ugly and traumatic things. To this day, one of my girlfriends still gets angry with me because, she says, "You don't remember anything!"

I attribute sketchy memory to traumas I experienced in my household as a child. I had three brothers who were all Scorpios. I don't know what it was about their sign that caused trouble in our lives, but these three males were the source of a whole lot of anguish. I now laugh at many of those childhood experiences, but going through them was anything but funny. I remember one particularly traumatic event, I said, "I wish there was a pill I could take to make me forget the bad stuff." I believe that was my first metaphysical approach to healing, as well as my first recognition that if I left the past where it was I could then look at each day brand new.

To this day, I believe it was this wish for a "forget pill" that's responsible for my poor memory. If an experience was bad, I have a hard time recounting it. Problem is, I also have difficulty remembering good experiences too! *"C'est la vie,"* as the French would say, "That's Life!" It comes with the territory I guess. There are many studies on children who have forgotten the traumas of their childhood. Some theories say traumas need to be rehashed if they are to be healed. So-called trauma experts might disagree with me, but if the mind knows to protect itself from bad memories by forgetting them, why in the world would we insist upon dredging them up again? If it's simply to look at it, and rewrite the story, then perhaps it's a worthwhile exercise.

FORGIVENESS IS THE FOUNTAIN OF YOUTH

I didn't begin my forgiveness practice knowing I would start looking younger and feel healthier. Actually, it took me a while to realize what was going on. But once I did, I jumped in with both feet. It was about then that I decided I wanted to teach the Power of Forgiveness and how it could enhance ones life and wellbeing. I noticed that every time I talked about forgiveness, I raised my vibration and I felt better. As well, I found I assisted those to whom I spoke about this power in emotional and spiritual healing. It felt so good to talk about and teach forgiveness that I wanted to do much more. Many of the people I ministered said they got "goose bumps" and experienced an elevation in their vibration. No matter whom we needed to forgive, all of us would walk away feeling better.

I also discovered that often what I thought was forgiveness was not necessarily forgiveness. And martyrdom was foolish, not forgiveness. Allowing someone to constantly hurt me was anything but forgiveness. Forgiveness, I realized, needed to start with me! When I started following and practicing the principles that I outline in this book it struck me that that I had stumbled upon an aphrodisiac. I started to love more easily. Consequently, I appreciated life more and knew how to simply be in the moment and *in-joy* life. Today I can now say I am *in-joy-in* my life!

The foundation for this book and much of my forgiveness work is *A Course in Miracles.* Many of you are familiar with ACIM because of Marianne Williamson, bestselling author of *A Return to Love.* I discovered the Course because the spiritual teachers I followed at the time mentioned it often. I remember listening to a Wayne Dyer CD; he referred to ACIM several times. Doreen Virtue mentioned it. These were two gurus that I respected, so I sought it out. I started studying the course in 2005, before I'd heard of Marianne. Someone saw my ACIM book and told me about her. I looked diligently for study groups.

I believe Spirit wanted me to learn this on my own and not be tainted by anyone else's opinions. After about a year in the course, I attended a retreat that Beverly Hutchinson McNeff did in Boston. While I was on the retreat, my dearest and best friend in the entire world had an aneurysm.

The Course helped me to deal with her death as well as perceive the world in a different light.

I recognize that *A Course in Miracles* can be a daunting read, and not everyone is drawn to it, so I am truly grateful that it brought me to this place. I share my learning with you because it transformed my life, and I believe it will transform yours as well. You will notice that I quote and refer to it often.

FORGIVENESS ILLUSTRATION

This story may help you appreciate the value of forgiveness:

> *Janice and her daughter Rachel are at a Broadway theatre to see The Lion King. This is Janice's first time seeing the production, and she is extremely excited that she was able to bring her ten-year-old daughter Rachel to enjoy it with her. Rachel has been singing the songs all week, and both of them are ecstatic to finally be in the theatre to see this beautiful production that they have heard so much about.*

> *When the procession begins and all the beautiful costumed characters come marching to the soulful African chants, Janice is immersed in it all and overcome by the beauty of the costumes and glorious music. Suddenly, out of nowhere the man sitting next to Janice gets up and hustles out*

of the theatre, stepping on her foot. The foot he stepped on is the one with the corn on it; Janice had been nursing that foot for days. Janice is furious. She can't imagine anything that could have called this man out so suddenly, and to add insult to injury he didn't even say "excuse me!"

Janice is so furious that she can no longer hear the exquisite music or see the beautiful costumes. Rachel has felt her mother's anguish, and because she is very sensitive to her mom's feelings, she too is distracted from the production. Janice huffs and cusses under her breath. Not only does her daughter hear and feel her mother's anger and distraction, the couple behind them hears Janice's colorful language. They feel the energy of Janice's anger and are now distracted too. Janice is bitter about her toe being trampled, and incensed that the man never stopped to apologize.

When the man returns Janice tells him what he'd done to her foot, and that he never bothered to apologize! The gentleman shrugs his shoulders and half-heartedly says he is sorry. Janice bitterness grows. She doesn't think of anything else throughout the rest of the production. Neither does Rachel enjoy the show because she feels her mom's wrath and has decided to be angry with her mother. Two $200 seats are wasted! Her mom swears this is the last time she will make a trip to Broadway! They both leave the theater unhappy.

Now let's do a re-write with a different ending:

Janice acknowledges the pain. Instead of holding onto anger she decides that NOTHING is going to keep her from this wonderful show that she and her daughter have planned all year to attend. She accepts that she has no clue as to what caused this man to jump up and rush from the theatre. Nor does it really matter. What matters is that she gets back to feeling good, and in a hurry, so that she can enjoy the show.

When her toe was stepped on, initially she was shocked and dismayed that someone had not only injured her but hadn't even bothered to acknowledge what he had done. Janice took three deep breaths, and then returned to appreciating the show. She delighted in the beautiful costumes and chants from the animals. Soon the pain subsided. She looked down at her lovely daughter—who too was briefly distracted by the incident—who was following her lead by refocusing her attention on the beautiful show before them. Rachel looks at her mom, and asks, "Are you all right Mommy?" Janice desires to honor her daughter and her feelings so she simply answers, "I will be all right."

Janice knows the importance of breathing so she takes three deep cleansing breaths to relax and ease the pain. In her breaths she visualizes her "attacker" as she bathes him in white light. This process only takes a few minutes.

Her pain vanishes. As she exhales she consciously releases any memory of the incident, anger and resentment. When the man returns she has just enough memory to remind her to keep her feet out of his way. Janice and Rachel leave the theatre singing, taking with them a lifetime of memories and joy of Rachel's first production, The Lion King.

THE BROADWAY SHOW IS YOUR LIFE!

Are you going to surrender peace and joy for memories of past pain and hurt? Or are you going to choose to release and let go and enjoy YOUR life? After all, this is YOUR LIFE! I don't want you to miss the beauty of life because of past hurts. You may be thinking, "Someone stepping on my toe isn't the same as being molested. It's not the same as someone bringing my career to a screeching halt. It's not the same as being betrayed by my spouse!" Or is it? If you are missing out on the Joy of Life is there really a difference in YOUR experience, and YOUR wellbeing?

This is YOUR LIFE! Don't miss the beauty of living because of a past hurt.

All Errors are Equal

*There is no order of difficulty in miracles. One is
not harder or bigger than another. They are all the same.
All expressions of love are maximal.*
- A Course in Miracles

Initially you may find it difficult to forgive. You may
think it unreasonable to forgive some people and situations. Before you give up, or decide against practicing
forgiveness, consider that there is nothing more important
than your happiness. Right now, if you are holding on to
the pain from the past then you have decided that your
happiness isn't paramount. Or perhaps you have decided
to find pleasure in pain. Know that that is what you are doing when you relive past hurts and resentments, when you
refuse to let go of the past. You may insist that you aren't
holding onto the past, you just refuse to forgive it. Or per-

haps you think you have let a situation go, but the memory of it still evokes an emotional response. Remember this rule of thumb, whenever you are questioning your need to forgive: *If you feel any attachment at all to an injury, a person, or a situation, then you must forgive.*

When you consider the hurtful acts that have been committed against you, I want you to think about what Jesus did when the woman who had committed adultery was brought to him. Jesus drew a circle and said, "He who is without sin, cast the first stone." Notice, Jesus didn't say, "If you've only told a little lie, then you may cast a stone." Nor did he tell the murderers, "You definitely can't cast a stone." Jesus told everyone present the same thing, "He who is without sin, cast the first stone." I believe Jesus deliberately chose not to make any distinctions in sins and people because all of us miss the mark. Jesus wants us to understand that all sin is the same and all healing is the same.

Illness comes from judgment. Healing comes from forgiveness. When we drop the stone rather than throw it we are saying NO to all conditions of hurt. We are applying the same forgiveness to the person who stepped on our toe, as we do to the person who molested us. We are saying YES to enjoying the show! That is, we agree, "There is no order of difficulty in miracles!" We recognize that the miracle is about a change in our perception. Yes, it really is that easy.

What Forgiveness Looks Like

Forgiveness means you have let go of the past and it has no impact or bind on your life now. Sure, you may have memories, but those memories are no longer emotionally charged. In later chapters we will explore how letting go of the past leads to breaking limiting, destructive patterns. The following quote has been attributed to Lily Tomlin and I believe it is a beautiful summation: "Forgiveness means giving up all hope of a better past." As I stated earlier, you will know you have forgiven when you are able to look back at a situation without any attachment to it. You will feel the same way about that situation as you do about yesterday's cup of coffee — nothing. It simply was.

Those situations to which you remain emotionally attached are the ones that you want to continue to work on. This is why forgiveness is an on-going process. When we look at the places in our life where we feel disconnected, we'll be able to see what or whom we need to forgive. This is why I insist that we have history to forgive as well as situations. Wherever you feel an emotional attachment, either in the form of sadness, remorse, pain, anger or guilt, you have a situation in need of healing.

> *I remember as a little girl hearing my aunt say men and women are different. A man could roll around in the gutter, get up and clean himself off and still be a man. But if a woman "slipped," she was no longer a lady when she got up. Think about that for a minute. That is a heavy burden for a girl to carry. I recognize that was a sign of the times and that my aunt meant well. Still, I have always been a free-spirited sort of girl. I always enjoyed the company of boys, from heavy petting to heavy kissing, and I lost my virginity*

*at a relatively early age. Through it all, some-
where embedded in my psyche was the thought
that I had slipped and fallen and so "I'm not a
lady." Of course, so the prevailing belief went,
"a lady" doesn't allow a boy to feel on her, even
if it feels good! This seemingly harmless belief of
my aunt's led to feelings of guilt and disconnect.
I am sure it affected my self-esteem and sense of
self worth when it came to men because I would
always short change myself in my choice of men.
As a matter of fact, when someone decent would
choose me I would be surprised because I didn't
think of myself as a real lady. It's hilarious,
because my daughters are the epitome of graceful-
ness; I would often wonder, "Who raised y'all?"
Of course I did, because I am a lady. No matter what my aunt thought about women who
"slipped." Of course my sexual energy had nothing at all to do with whether or not I was a lady.
I was just a frisky, sexual girl!*

This is an example of a situation that I needed to
forgive. I was never upset with my aunt. I laugh when I remember hearing her say that, and totally understand where
she was coming from at the time. Her position doesn't
bother me. It's okay for her, and it worked for her. And
yet, her words, at least for me, were more than a harmless
comment. Those words were embedded in me. I needed to
look at how it shaped me as a woman, and forgive them,
so that I could grow my sense of self worth, clear that I am
a beautiful woman, lady, goddess, with all the attributes

of beautiful femininity and yin energy. Whether or not I let my boyfriend feel me up. Whether or not I lost my virginity at sixteen, I'm perfectly good and fine and I look upon that past as a wonderful old movie. Accepting every bit about the experience. From how I felt about it, to how others reacted to me. And I bless it. I embrace it. I even cherish it. Now when I look back on old boyfriends, and my so-called "slip-ups," which allegedly kept me from being a lady, I realize I'm "all good" and absolutely perfect. Henry, the first boy who gave me an orgasm, who, as I later found out, had friends waiting to get their turn, is nothing but a character in my old movie. My loving past has given me a great story to tell. I bless Henry, and the others.

Take a moment to think of a situation, perhaps one you have never considered significant but could be coloring the view you have of yourself today.

What was the situation?

_____

_____

_____

_____

_____

_____

_____

_____

_____

_____

How do you believe it has impacted your life?

_____

_____

_____

_____

_____

_____

_____

_____

_____

What do you think it may have kept you from being, doing, having?

_____

_____

_____

_____

_____

_____

_____

_____

_____

_____

If you choose to forgive and let it go, what do you think
would change in your life? What might be possible for you?

_____

_____

_____

_____

_____

_____

_____

_____

_____

_____

_____

_____

_____

_____

_____

_____

_____

The Road to BLISS

Extreme happiness. The ecstasy of salvation. Spiritual joy.
~ This Is Bliss

We are going to take a trip down a road that you may have never imagined traveling. I may say some things that make you uncomfortable and introduce you to ideas that you have never considered before. I believe, however, these ideas are already in you, consequently your spirit will recognize them and appreciate what they mean to your joy and bliss in this lifetime.

The following exercise will help you see why you should explore these outrageous ideas. It should answer the questions, What's in it for me? Why bother? Forgiveness is the greatest gift you can give yourself. By practicing forgiveness, you improve your personal relationships, as well as casual contacts and acquaintances. But, YOU, my dear, are the primary beneficiary, and I am hoping that you accept that for yourself. To do that, take a moment and reflect and rate yourself on the following:

Bliss is defined as:[1]

n.

1. Extreme happiness; ecstasy.

2. The ecstasy of salvation; spiritual joy.

blissed out *Slang*

To go into a state of ecstasy.

On a scale of one to ten, rate yourself in the following categories, with ten as the absolute highest. For example, on the Bliss Scale, a one means "I rarely feel bliss." A ten would indicate, "I always feel like I am in a joyful, blissful state; if life were any better I would physically be walking on clouds."

On health, a one would be "I am always sick or feeling poorly." A ten is, "I could jog several miles, I am extremely energetic, and I never ever get sick and I am at the perfect weight."

---

1   www.thefreedictionary.com

BLISS LEVEL CHECK-UP

Family Relationships

1   2   3   4   5   6   7   8   9   10

Intimate Relationships

1   2   3   4   5   6   7   8   9   10

Sex

1   2   3   4   5   6   7   8   9   10

Health

1   2   3   4   5   6   7   8   9   10

Physical Appearance

1   2   3   4   5   6   7   8   9   10

Work

1   2   3   4   5   6   7   8   9   10

Finances

1   2   3   4   5   6   7   8   9   10

Spiritual Well-Being

1   2   3   4   5   6   7   8   9   10

Emotional Well-Being

1   2   3   4   5   6   7   8   9   10

Overall Bliss Level

1   2   3   4   5   6   7   8   9   10

Now, be honest with yourself. Do you think 10s in all areas is a possibility for you? Are you afraid of experiencing a 10 in any area? How do you imagine life would be if you were a 10 in all categories? How would it affect those around you? I am willing to bet that you have decided that a 10 is not for you in some areas. That's okay. I'm also willing to bet that some of you think others will be negatively impacted if you walked around feeling good all the time. That's okay too. We'll explore that, and then we shall see if others are able to grow from your bliss, or if your joy would stunt their growth.

I know this is important since most of us aren't willing to be in a perpetual state of joy because we mistakenly believe that crying with the rest of the world is somehow cool. I mean, if your girlfriend calls to complain about her love life then you don't want to be in a good mood about yours do you? That would be cruel; to be in bliss about your love life while your best friend is having trouble with her relationship. But what if your appreciation for your love life could help your friend appreciate hers? What if she understood that when she spoke with you that her positive vibrations multiplied because you take her to joyful places? What if she came to depend on you for that? Would that be a bad thing?

Wouldn't it be worth the work if you went up several points in the area of health, because you were practicing forgiveness and living in the moment? What if your risk for cancer could completely vanish and your arthritis could disappear? And it all happened simply because you practiced forgiveness and learned to look at every situation in a new light. Do you think your friends would want a piece of what you have? Might they want to change their life?

Of course we may have some people to leave and never return. We need to accept the fact that not everyone wants to live a blissful life. Some people have made a decision to live painful, unfulfilled lives. Here's my question to you, what do *you* want?

MY HAPPINESS IS MY GREATEST GIFT TO OTHERS!

I have a girlfriend who, no matter when we talk, has the same story. I believe we're meant to be lifelong friends, but this woman, who I'll call Cheryl, always has a boatload of problems! Her mother has Alzheimer's, so she has to give up her life for her mother. Her grandmother was grossly ill, so she had to leave a house that she loved to move closer to her. Her sister had serious financial issues, so she needed to sacrifice to help her out. Her son had marital problems, so she needed to bail him out some mess. Needless to say, Cheryl was never in good health. Nor could she ever find time to play or let loose and enjoy life. I'm convinced that this is what she wants. That is, she decided that in this lifetime she wants to be a martyr.

Now, I realize our families can have a multitude of issues. But if you are always bailing family out of this or that, then know that you are choosing this. When do you say, enough is enough, I need to take care of me? This is where we must let go, forgive them, forgive the situation, and forgive ourselves. Here's where we get to embrace our love of self and create a new vision for our life. When we do, the miracles begin to unfold.

The miracle is that you heal others when you go to your place of joy. Let's look at Cheryl's situation and see how forgiveness might help her. What or who should Cheryl forgive? I don't know what kind of childhood she had but let's say from an early age Cheryl assumed the role of the parent and became the primary caretaker. What if her mother dropped the ball, leaving Cheryl with the task of parenting herself and her siblings? Or perhaps her mother used guilt to get Cheryl to behave in certain ways, so now Cheryl takes on other people's problems because it makes her feel better about herself. If that is the case, Cheryl needs to go to a place of forgiveness of her family. She would accept the role that was assigned to her then work to let it go. Let it go in love and compassion. Let it go as she creates for herself a brand new vision for her life. While doing so, recognizing that she may never fully understand why her family put that burden on her.

Because Cheryl let go, she now leads a healthier, happier life. She is now showing her family how to enjoy life, and thus has become a source of inspiration and anchor. Her sister feels her vibration and starts feeling better about herself and life. Cheryl's newfound energy is contagious. Her daughter ceases to whine because her mother has more energy to play games with her. Even the store clerk recognizes Cheryl's glow. As a result, the clerk has a better day, and enjoys her life more. The store clerk goes home happier and her children are beneficiaries of this increased happiness. All of this because Cheryl forgave, let the past go, and decided to live a happier, more blissful life!

It's All a Reflection

*When you meet anyone, remember it is a holy
encounter. As you see him, you will see yourself.
As you treat him, you will treat yourself. As you
think of him, you will think of yourself.*
~ A Course in Miracles

Challenging situations are opportunities to turn within and forgive you! They take us to places within that are in need of forgiveness; places we imagined were already healed. I had a situation at a Maryland restaurant that caused me to revisit something I thought I had let go of. Something I'd failed to truly acknowledge and forgive.

*On a recent visit to Ledo's Restaurant I ordered a
salad with extra dressing and breadsticks. When
I got my bill, I noticed it cost more than the un-*

limited soup, salad and breadsticks. I pointed this out to the waitress and asked her to change my bill. She told me that since I ordered the items a la carte they were more expensive. I figured she was new, therefore wasn't able to change the bill. I asked for the manager, whom I was sure would be more than willing to make me happy. The unlimited soup, salad and breadsticks were $6.99. The salad (not unlimited), breadsticks and extra dressing came to $9.99. The manager appeared. I asked her kindly to reduce my bill. She said, "You didn't order the soup, salad and breadsticks, so I can't change your order." "So, let me understand this," I stated, "had I eaten all the salad I wanted, and all the breadsticks I could stomach and consumed all the soup in the world it would have been cheaper than one bowl of soup, an extra side of dressing, and an order of breadsticks?"

"Yes," she answered.

So I replied, "Okay, then I'm changing my order. Give me a bowl of soup!"

The manager put her hands on her hips and demanded, "Are you going to eat the soup?" I burst out laughing. All right, now this is getting out of hand. I swept my hand across the room and asked, "Is this something you ask ALL of your patrons?" Never had I been asked if I was going to actually eat what I ordered, so long as I paid for it. I was forced to order the soup to get the cheaper price! And no, I didn't eat the soup because at the time I was refraining from meat.

TWO WEEKS LATER

Two weeks later I had a taste for a Ledo salad. This time I knew to order the unlimited soup, salad and breadsticks and I would simply ask the waiter to hold the soup. I smiled at the waiter, and asked if she remembered me. Of course she did, and, she said, she would be sure to place the order as unlimited soup, salad and breadsticks. Good. I was hungry and I could hardly wait to dig into my salad. A few minutes later my order arrived. There was just one little problem; the salad was frozen! Yes, frozen, hard as a block of ice.

Two men sat across from me and their meals had been delivered to them at the same time. I went over to one gentleman and inquired about his salad. He hadn't started eating it yet, but said he didn't think it was frozen. It was cold, but not frozen. When the waitress walked by, I showed her my salad, which could be scooped up at once, since it was clumped together.

"Not a problem," she stated, "I will get you another salad."

"Great," I said. Fifteen minutes later she still hadn't delivered the salad. I finally told her never mind, forget about it. I stood up to leave and the manager, who two weeks ago had demanded to know if I was going to eat soup I was paying for, was hot on my heels! She was yelling, "You can't leave, you haven't paid for your salad!"

I laughed. "It was frozen! I don't want a frozen salad. The waitress saw it was frozen, and you guys never brought a replacement." She threatened to get the police. Police were in the restaurant at the time, so she didn't have to go far. Now, I'm usually very outspoken and courageous about things like this, but I didn't want to cause a scene in the restaurant.

So I walked over to the officers and asked them, "Are you going to arrest me because I didn't pay for a frozen salad." The female officer nodded yes. "I don't believe this!" Finally, the manager decided she would charge me half price. I paid the half price and left a tip for the waiter.

After I paid my tab, the gentleman who got his salad when I got mine signaled to the manager to come over. I followed her to his table because I knew without a doubt that his salad was also frozen. He told the manager he wasn't going to pay for his salad because it was frozen. "Okay," she said, "I'll take it off your bill."

Can you imagine my outrage when that happened? By this time any coolness I possessed was totally gone. "Oh, no she didn't!" I stood in the middle of the restaurant with my hands outstretched and loudly exclaimed, "I need someone to explain to me what just happened here! Why is it that we both ordered salads, I had to pay for mine and he didn't? We both had frozen salads! What's going on here?"

One of the officers approached and asked me to quiet down. I said, "But you were going to arrest me for not paying for a salad, and he gets his free!" The officer said, "I didn't tell you I would arrest you. The female officer said she would." He asked me to come outside with him, so I that I could calm down. Then he asked me what happened. He was surprised once he heard the details and said he would go in with me to try and get my money back. Finally, I realized it wasn't worth it, that I was attaching too much significance to a few dollars. I was ready to go to war over a principle!

I calmed down, walked over to the manager and said, "I forgive you. I know you wouldn't want someone to treat your mother like that." She said I caused a scene the last time I was in there because I wanted to pay less than the meal cost and that she saw a pattern with me. In essence, she was holding a grudge against me. As I left she asked me to never set foot in the restaurant again.

What a crazy experience. Later, I realized I needed to take a close look at that situation. After all, I'm a metaphysician who regularly practices forgiveness. Why did I choose to have this experience, right when I was in the middle of doing a video series on forgiveness? I'm always accountable, right? I believe in the Law of Attraction. I also believe all situations should be forgiven and are a reflection of something we hold within. Well, when I peeled back this situation I could see what I had done to attract it. More importantly, I realized I needed to forgive myself, which is the starting point for all forgiveness work. Because we're so connected to each other, when we forgive ourselves, we are also forgiving others.

It took me a day or so to see I had behaved in a similar manner several years earlier. While a manager for SuperMedia I had a client who did a direct mail postcard campaign with us. The client, whom I'll call Carl, happened to be my personal painter; and he was also African-American. I was confident that a direct mail campaign would help generate business for him, so I convinced him to purchase direct mail cards from us. Since I was a manager, I had one of my sales reps take the account and set up Carl's campaign. The cards went out without the client's prior approval of them, before he could make any needed changes. After the cards had been mailed, Carl came into our office; upset about the artwork as well as the offer. I must admit, Carl could take two hours to tell a ten-minute story and I was impatient with him.

Rather than offer to provide additional cards for free, and "eat" the error, I told Carl I was sorry but there was nothing I could do for him. Actually, I could have given him a free campaign or an adjustment on his bill. But I didn't. I think my knowing him was why I refused to give him the adjustment and service he deserved. Like Carl and me, the manager at Ledo's was African American. Was she, like me, taking liberties because we both were African American? Rather than valuing me as a customer, one worthy of quality service, perhaps this manager thought I should tolerate poor service, perhaps the same way I felt Carl should accept mediocre service.

I also wondered if I went back to further aggravate her and myself because I hadn't forgiven or gotten over the first visit. There were at least three possible scenarios playing out which contributed to me having this experience:

1. At the time, I was doing a video series on forgiveness. I tend to feel this work is very easy, when in fact it can be difficult. I invited this experience so I could remember the pain of un-forgiveness in a situation that needed forgiveness, and so I could have a story to share,

2. Although it had been several years ago, I could readily recall a situation that I handled similarly. Carl was as upset about what occurred as I had been. He also probably felt as betrayed as I did.

3. I did not get over the first visit when I was charged more for the salad. So my soul wanted to repeat the exercise so I could truly "get over it."

I needed this opportunity so I could look back and forgive myself, and, if possible, to even go to Carl and ask for his forgiveness. I discovered that I had never addressed the situation with Carl and I was harboring ill feelings towards myself, which was reflected back to me from the Ledo's manager. If I continued to harbor resentment and anger for the manager, then I would need to harbor resentment and anger for myself. I can't do that to me. I like myself too much to be angry with me.

I needed to find the humor in the situation, and to forgive the manager because it was a reflection of me! On the other hand, if I continued to talk about how horrible this person was, essentially I was talking about how horrible I am. These are not good feelings, and remember there is nothing more important than that "I" feel good. How can I feel good when I am condemning someone who is a reflection of me? I can't. I must forgive myself, and in order to forgive myself, I need to forgive others. And the reverse is true. In order to forgive them, I need to forgive me. This way we all are free.

A side note, the remark I made to the manager, "I forgive you," was not forgiveness. It was my attempt at showing her "I'm better than you because I can rise above this situation." This is a far cry from true forgiveness. True forgiveness means I have released her in my mind from any anger, resentment or grudges. I see her as a "Perfect Child of God." I can look back on the situation without regret or emotional attachment. Besides, the manager didn't seek forgiveness from me, so it was not my place to attempt to make her feel as if she did with my "I forgive you" comment. In fact, what I was really trying to do was make her feel guilty, while attempting to make myself feel better!

Release All Judgment

*You have no idea of the tremendous release and
deep peace that comes from meeting yourself and
your brothers totally without judgment.*
- A Course in Miracles

judg·ment[2]
1. an act or instance of judging
2. the ability to judge, make a decision, or form an
   opinion objectively, authoritatively, and wisely,
   especially in matters affecting action; good sense;
   discretion: *a man of sound judgment.*
3. the demonstration or exercise of such ability or
   capacity: *The major was decorated for the judgment
   he showed under fire.*
4. the forming of an opinion, estimate, notion, or

---

[2] www.thefreedictionary.com

conclusion, as from circumstances presented to the mind: *Our judgment as to the cause of his failure must rest on the evidence.*

5. the opinion formed: *He regretted his hasty judgment.*

For purposes of forgiveness, we are going to redefine the word "judgment." Judgment in this context doesn't mean to apply "good sense." That would be discernment. For example, should I step out into the street on a red light, when good judgment or discernment tell me to cross on green? Discernment means we are assessing a situation and making a wise call. Judgment, on the other hand, is always negative. It is putting someone or something or some event in an unfavorable light.

From this perspective, when we speak of judgment we are talking about forming an opinion as to why someone made a particular decision. Why someone treated you poorly. When we judge, we condemn another for his or her "sins" and wrongdoings towards us. Consequently, the way we look at judgment will be more in alignment with condemnation. However, I want to continue to use the word judgment so that we appreciate that we are forming an opinion, however, *we DO NOT have enough information to do so.*

As you may have guessed, I love Broadway. One of my favorite Broadway productions is *Wicked,* that tells the story of the horrible green wicked witch of the west, and how she became evil. I believe it is a wonderful example of why we shouldn't judge. We have been condemning this poor "wicked" witch ever since we saw the movie *The Wizard of Oz.* But this story tells us what really happened, and from it we are able to see that we lack sufficient information to deem her wicked. That's all I'll tell you about the play. To know more, you must go see the show or read the book!!

con·demn [k*uh* n-**dem**]³
verb (used with object)
1. to express an unfavorable or adverse judgment on; indicate strong disapproval of; censure.
2. to pronounce to be guilty; sentence to punishment: *to condemn a murderer to life imprisonment.*
3. to give grounds or reason for convicting or censuring: *His acts condemn him.*
4. to judge or pronounce to be unfit for use or service: *to condemn an old building*

> *Whenever the pain of guilt seems to ATTRACT*
> *you, remember that if you yield to it, you are*
> *deciding AGAINST your happiness.*
> *~ A Course in Miracles*

In order to discuss judgment, we must first examine self-judgment. Do you realize you are connected with everyone you encounter? If your upbringing was Christian, then you know Jesus said God is his father and that we are all brothers. Which means you and I are cut from the same mold. We are interconnected. The way I perceive you is the way I perceive myself. I can't help it because of our connection. So whether you realize it or not, when you are judging me you are judging yourself.

---

3   www.thefreedictionary.com

Look at your life. What do you have a hard time embracing? Is it relationships? How do you judge others who stay in what you perceive as bad relationships? Do you have a hard time with food? How do you perceive others who you think are out of shape or overweight? Are you afraid to speak in public? How do you look at others who are public speakers?

Wherever you are critical and condemning, is a place for self-healing. I can't help but reflect back on the movie *American Beauty*. Do you remember how Chris Cooper, who played the role of Colonel Frank Fitts, was really upset about homosexuality? He was a true homophobic. Well, it turns out he had homosexual tendencies. He hated homosexuals because he hated that within himself!

At this point you may be ready to put this book down and say enough is enough! You may say, for example, "I abhor rapist and there is nothing in me that could have that tendency, so I have every right to condemn or judge." Well think about it. What does a rapist do? He overpowers and takes advantage of someone else. He exerts his power, and makes them succumb to him. Look in your life. Have you ever exerted your power? Have you ever taken advantage of someone else? Perhaps in negotiating a better price for something, you lied that someone offered you a better deal so the person you want to do business with would give you a lesser price. That could be considered taking advantage. My point is, we all have our shortcomings, and just as Jesus never assigned degrees to sin neither should we. As a matter of fact, Jesus simply told the adulterer "go and sin no more."

I recognize this may be a hard pill to swallow especially if you or someone close to you has experienced molestation, abuse rape. Please note that I am in no way being cavalier about these subjects, and it is not my desire to lack compassion either. I am simply pointing out that in all areas we have equal or similar tendencies. So this means all of us have "fallen short" as we travel this journey. All of us have committed sin. And do you know what the meaning of "sin" is? To sin means to "miss the mark." All of us have missed the mark at some point.

Again, to keep us on track and to prevent you from throwing this book and these ideas away, I want you to understand that I do believe if and when we serve as jurors or we are specifically called to judge, then we need to do so. But if you haven' t been called to judge, do you really need to wallow in it? Do you need to Facebook the horrors, call your friends and share the horror stories over and over again? If you believe at all in the Law of Attraction and that your "happiness is your greatest gift to others," then you know that doing any of the above things increases your chances of experiencing them again and again, emotionally or physically!

As a side note, I would like to add that if you happen to work with a group or organization that offers support or has programs designed to prevent painful things from happening to people, I applaud you. I am grateful for your work. It is much needed. Let's say you are working with a group that seeks to prevent domestic violence against women, then consider calling your group "Promoting Peace & Love" for women. This is healthier and much more beneficial than a group called "Preventing Domestic Violence" for these words actually call forth violence rather than alleviate it because our words have creative power.

The words peace and love call forth peace and love and help group members cultivate and maintain a more peaceful frame of mind, while doing the work. Hence, the group is more effective because it is calling forth all that is good, Peace and Love.

So how does this relate to judgment? When I condemn you, I am really condemning myself. So why don't I forgive you, and then this will allow me to be forgiven? "Forgive us our trespasses, as we forgive those who trespass against us," says the Lord's Prayer.

Jesus taught us to release judgment because he recognized that judgment keeps us from seeing the Kingdom of God within. Jesus did not put any degrees of sin or "missing the mark" on any of us. Rather, he did quite the opposite. No one was left to condemn the woman. He looked up and asked her, "is there no one here to condemn you?" She answered, "no." Jesus then told her that her sins had been forgiven, and to "Go and sin no more."

Now really, do you believe that Jesus thought for one minute that this woman would not "miss the mark" or "sin" again? What he knew and what he saw was her perfection. Telling her to go and sin no more meant she was free from the past. And all those who left, who knew they could not cast a stone against her were free as well. There was no magic water that Jesus put on the woman. He didn't even give her a special prayer. He simply said, "Go and sin no more." He released her from the past, a power that we all have. That is, all of us have the "magical" ability to release others and ourselves from the past. As we let others off the hook, we also free ourselves of condemnation and judgment.

EVERY OPPORTUNITY TO FORGIVE SOMEONE ELSE IS AN OPPORTUNITY FOR SELF-FORGIVENESS!

This cannot be emphasized enough. We are all related. Everyone is a mirror image of us. We are connected because we are all cut from the same Divine Cloth. Whenever someone in your life irritates you, they are there because you invited them so you can have that experience. YES, even relatives. Even your parents. There were millions of people to choose from when you decided to make your entrance onto this planet. You specifically chose the parents that you did because you desired to have the experience that only they could provide. And since we are blessed with the beautiful gift of choice, you also get to make different choices along the way.

You might ask, How can I possibly change my parents? And my siblings? They are with me for life, right? Correct, they are with you for life, but you can change them. You do this by changing your perception of them. And when you change your perception of them, you are at the same time releasing yourself!

If your parents bother you with their drinking, because they both are alcoholics, when you free them and forgive them because of who they are, you have just released yourself. Perhaps you aren't an alcoholic but you are chronically late! Well, you have just freed yourself from punishment and judgment because you have released and freed your parents. This works with everyone you free. You allow them to be who they are. You view them in another light. You view them as the Perfect Light of God. *And now that you* acknowledge that even with their frailties they are the Perfect Light of God, you have made the same statement for yourself. Isn't that a joyful occurrence? A blissful thought?

I have had clients who don't judge others nearly as harshly as they judge themselves. They will give others permission to mess up, but they won't permit themselves to make any errors. I find this to be especially true for people who are afraid to speak in front of others. They fear being judged, even though they aren't harsh on other presenters. The same rule applies. *As you are free yourself, you free others!*

If you can see your brother merits pardon, you have learned forgiveness is your right as much as his. Nor will you think that God intends for you a fearful judgment that your brother does not merit. For it is the truth that you can merit neither more nor less than he.
- A Course in Miracles

Release the Past

Time can release as well as imprison. You anticipate the future on the basis of your past experience, and plan for it accordingly.

Yet by doing so you are aligning past and future, and not allowing the miracle, which would intervene between them, to free you to be born again.

The miracle enables you to see your brother without his past, and so perceive him as born again. Your past was made in anger, and if you use it to attack the present, you will not see the freedom that the present holds.

Look lovingly upon the present, for it holds the only things that are forever true.
- A Course in Miracles

When I hold onto the past, I am holding myself hostage. When I hold myself hostage, then I am holding everyone else I encounter hostage with me. Let's take a look at how this applies to us with our everyday life. And of course we can always look at how it applies to us in relationships.

When we reflect on what I encountered at Ledo's Restaurant, there are several ways I could have interpreted what happened. In looking at my interpretations, they could impact my future and how I view pizza, restaurants, waiters, and managers. I could have decided that this particular Ledo has horrible service, and that I will never eat there again. I could have decided that ALL Ledo restaurants have horrendous service; I will never eat at ANY of them again. I could have concluded that all pizza restaurants are awful and the service is terrible so I'll never eat at another pizza restaurant again. I might have said, "all black managers and waitresses provide terrible service and if I get a black waitress or manager I will leave the restaurant.

Now, look at all of the things I *could* have missed because of this one experience. Isn't this what we do all of the time with the past, events, people and situation? As you read my "could have" list you may have thought it is absolutely absurd to go that far and deep because of one little experience. Well, isn't that what we do all the time? How often have we stereotyped an entire race of people because of one or two experiences with members from that race or because of a past experience? I even hear people stereotyping cities. This is easy to do when we bring our past into our present!

If you're a woman, perhaps you are reluctant to have a relationship with another man because of a past relationship. Maybe you have been "burned" more than once in your relationships. So now, is it fair to bring your hurts and fears into your present? How about if it happens ten times with ten different men? Is it now safe to say all men are jerks, dogs, abusers, cheaters? I guess it is if you don't mind missing the bliss of having a beautiful relationship with a wonderful man?

What happens when you change your perception and you look lovingly upon the present? When you release others from the past, you allow your perception of them to change, and in changing your perception YOU change, which means the men you attract change as well! It takes knowing who you are to know who your brother is. I must be really clear that I am a divine reflection of all that is good, in order for me to recognize in you "all that is good." If I am harboring bitterness and resentment towards myself, then it is absolutely impossible for me to release you from any past. This is why self-forgiveness is so important.

How Do I Recognize My Divinity?

In order to really practice forgiveness, I must believe in some sort of Higher Power. Some form of creation. Even if you don't believe in God I hope you have accepted the fact that there was a collective consciousness of some magnificent power that started all of this. Let's say this power that started this came from Divine Love. Most religions agree that God ultimately is a God of Love. If we came from that Higher Power, from that Source, and we are created in Its image, then that must mean we embody the attributes of all that is Good. When we determine that there is an all-encompassing "all good," then what can be its opposite? That which is not good! But wait a minute, if we are created from that which is all-good, then ALL good can have no opposite! ALLNESS constitutes ALL. So that must be the truth of who I am. Therefore, "I am All Good!"

Now, if I am all-good then that must mean anyone who was created from this Divine Source is also all good. But how can we be good when so many bad things are happening? Well, again, only one thing can be certain. The only thing real is Love. So that means everything else is an illusion.

This is how the Miracle begins to unfold. Acceptance of your divinity helps you to recognize the absolute truth of who you are. Now what do you choose to focus on? The fact that you told a lie or the absolute truth, which is, that you are perfect? Which one puts you in denial? If you negate either one, then you are in denial. The real question is, which one brings you greater peace? Of course you should feel better when you recognize the absolute truth of who you are. If you are not feeling better, it is because you are keeping the overriding fact that you tell lies in the forefront. Yes, you may have told a lie. But in this moment, in this second, in this Holy Instant, is where the truth of who you are resides.

How can you negate that truth because of a past thought or action? How does that take away from the very fact, that at this moment, this second, this Holy Instant, "you are perfect?" Because it is in the Holy Instant where your perfection lies. And this is where we always want to reside. As we take our Holy Instant with us, as we live in the Holy Instant, we will embrace a more Blissful Journey of Life.

We can't go alone; we must bring our brother along with us. In this instant, this very instant, in between the "lies" lives the truth of who our brother is. As we free him, we free ourselves and achieve atonement. At-one-ment! We can live in the oneness of our goodness whenever we choose. This is one reason we meditate, to come back to that oneness. So how outside of meditation do we bring this goodness to light?

RELEASE YOURSELF

I release myself from the past! I do not hold myself hostage to the fact that I was once unfair to a customer. That is not the truth of who I am. I acknowledge and affirm the truth of who I am: I AM PERFECT because I am created in the Image of Perfection. The fact remains that I did treat my brother unfairly. So what do I do? I can face it and look at it and acknowledge, and apologize to all those I have impacted. I can do that with compassion and sincerity. All the while remembering who I am. And this frees me to live in the present! This is true repentance!

It is like watching a movie. There I was, acting unjustly to a customer. Wow, that was not cool. I want to live in the present, but with compassion I want to release what I did in the past. I am able to look at that past as an impartial third party, knowing that is not the truth of who I am. Without fear, I am able to call and apologize for my past wrongdoings. And because I can look at it, and know that it is not the truth of who I am, I am able to act in the present accordingly with all future situations regarding customers. Do you see how that works?

If I hold myself hostage to the past, and look at myself with shortcomings and failures, then apparently I am setting myself up for future shortcomings and failures. If I look at myself as the image of Perfection, now I am able to free myself to act accordingly. I know this to be true of whom I am. So what happens when I slip up? I repeat the process all over again!

Remember, what is true for me is true for you. This is how, when I am in my Christ consciousness, I approach all things. So now I need to apply this to the Ledo manager. She is perfect. She is Divine. She is the image of Divine Creation. This is the truth of who she is no matter what the situation may have shown me. So now that I have released her from the past, I have released what is tied to that situation from my present. I am free to enjoy pizza. I am free to enjoy pizza from Ledo. I am free to enjoy black waitresses. I am free to enjoy meals at restaurants that have black managers. I may deem this particular manager not ready yet and that's okay. As long as I keep in my mind and memory that she is perfect. It becomes more likely that if I keep this truth uppermost in my mind, I could have a divine experience at that restaurant and with *her*.

It simply takes me having made up in my mind the truth, to see her with the absolute truth. *This is how the miracle unfolds and bliss levels are raised!*

EXERCISE IN RELEASING THE PAST

Please make sure you are in a meditative state when you do this exercise. You may choose to wear white, light a candle and put on some soft, New Age music, or any meditation music that will allow your chakras to open. Begin this exercise with a prayer of intent. Let Spirit/Source/God/Mother/Father God know that it is your desire to remove all blocks to unforgiveness so that you live a more Blissful Life. Invite the angels to join in on the session with you, to guide you to open your heart and mind to complete this exercise.[4]

Step 1

Pick a situation where someone, or something, has offended you. It could be a person, a situation, an event, or even history. At the top of the page write "The Situation," or "The Event." Detail the atrocities that were committed against you. Be as specific as you can. Now hold the paper between both hands, and gently breathe in the details of what occurred to you. Feel the breath through your hands as it resonates with your heart. Sit with it for a few minutes.

Step 2

Open the paper, and now write where you have committed the same or similar atrocities. If someone has lied on you, reflect on when you told a lie. In the case of murder, you may simply reflect on when you have killed any

---

4   These directions will be noted in each of the exercises that I suggest. This is a reminder for you that whenever you do the exercises you want to be in a clear meditative state to gain the most benefit from the exercise.

living being, even if it was a mouse or roach. Or perhaps you killed someone's spirit with your words. Take the time to reflect on an atrocity that has the same characteristics that you have committed.

Step 3

Now gently fold the paper, and hold it in your hands. Again, breathe in the details of the atrocities. Breathe them in through your hands and feel it going to your heart. Feel the images as they go to your third eye, then to your crown. Allow this image to flow throughout your body. Bring it back down through each of your chakras. Feel it as it goes to your throat chakra, your heart chakra, and down to your solar plexus. Feel it as it moves throughout your body. Sit in it and breathe in the essence of the atrocities. Feel it as it cascades through your sacral chakra and down to your root chakra.

As it cascades, allow Spirit to transform both atrocities into one, so that you don't see a distinction between the two. As you breathe it in, allow Spirit to transform the image into white light. Imagine this white light feels like Love. Embrace it, along with someone you truly love. This Spirit may be Jesus. It may be a baby, or it may be a best friend. As best as you can, allow this image to be the image of someone you hold in pure love. Let their light of love shine in this atrocity, and allow this powerful light to dissolve these memories for you.

The white light has now overtaken both atrocities and turned them into pure love. If you are in a quiet meditative space, Sprit will dissolve it and show you that it is but the past. It is an illusion for you and for your "enemy." Both of the situations have now been transformed into love, and dissolved into the permanency of yesterday.

Step 4

Now breathe in and free yourself. Gently open your hands and blow on the paper as a demonstration that it is now gone with the wind. As you free and release yourself from this past, you are also freeing the one you held a grievance against. Both of you are now free. You have released the past and you have let it go. You are now safe in the Holy Instant. You may burn the paper, shred it or even flush it down the toilet. No matter what you decide to do with the paper, you have now freed yourself and released your brother. Both of you are free. Repeat this exercise as often as necessary to release you from any past situations.

One of the benefits of practicing forgiveness, you'll find, is that you don't offend as easily. It doesn't mean you become a martyr. You will simply notice that you have fewer situations where people attempt to take advantage of you, and you will also find that less than well meaning people easily leave your life. You will attract more loving people into your life, people who have your best interest at heart, and people who respect you.

Living in the Present

*The past is but an illusion. There is no way I can go
back and grab what happened yesterday, or even a
minute ago. This lets me know that the past is not
real. Today I choose to look on the "Holy Instant" as
my only truth. In this Instant is my true Joy!*
~ This Is Bliss

Remember the graph you completed at the beginning
of the book, where you rated your Bliss Level. Undoubtedly
there were areas in which you had less than a ten, and in
some of these areas you may even think it is not possible to
get a ten. Let's take a trip down the road of *"I always get
my heart's desires."* Where do you think this road would
lead you?

Have you given up on your desires and dreams because
of fear of disappointment? Have you been told your desires

and dreams are too big or unrealistic. Have you been too concerned with and about other people to focus on your own needs and desires? Or maybe the many naysayers in your world have you afraid to take risk. Or, perhaps you are surrounded by underachievers, and you play small so you won't stand out in the crowd and be perceived as "The Uppity Big Dreamer."

It doesn't matter which of the categories your dashed dreams have fallen into. On this path of *"I always get my hearts desires"* we are going to look at our dreams exactly that way—as if they always come true. You know when we always get our heart's desires, right? We get our heart's desires when we become unafraid to dream and hope because we have *forgiven* all, including ourselves. And because we acknowledge our connection to Source, our heart's desires are always for our Highest Good.

So as you are making your way through your forgiveness journal, don't forget these people or situations that you may need to forgive:

FEAR OF DISAPPOINTMENT

Look at areas in your life where you have experienced disappointment trying to realize your dream. Was it in a relationship? Was it in a job? Was it in an acting role that you know you should have gotten? Make note of what your disappointments in life were. No matter how major or insignificant they may seem, anything that you attempted but failed to achieve will often leave you feeling disappointed.

EXERCISE FOR FORGIVING: FEAR OF DISAPPOINTMENT

Now that you have identified the areas where there is disappointment, think about the fear that was surrounding it before you started. Once you have identified the fear, then look at what may have caused the so-called failure. Was it your performance? Was it someone else? Or was it that you didn't really go after it because you were immobilized by fear.

Once you have identified what caused the disappointment, I want you to look at what came out of not getting what you wanted. Perhaps it was an "ideal" job that you didn't get. Where would you be if you had gotten the job? And what part of your life would be different if you had gotten the job? For example, perhaps you would not have met your child's father, and your son, who is the light of your world, would not have been born. Celebrate that which came out of your disappointment.

Get excited for all the wonderful things that happened because of what you wanted didn't happen. Now that you have done that, can you forgive what appeared as disappointment? Can you see there is always a happy outcome, so that now there is nothing to fear because everything always works out perfectly? Simple technique, but it's one we fail to use, and will off-handedly talk about, but seldom do we take the time to celebrate an unforeseen outcome because of a so-called failure.

Buy a cake, open a bottle of wine, throw a party, put on your favorite music and celebrate the beautiful outcomes *because* of a so-called failure. Adopt a mantra or affirmation that affirms, *"I am always successful."* My favorite mantra is, "I have the Midas touch and everything I touch turns to gold!"

> *God promises a happy outcome to everything.*
> *His promises make no exception.*
> *- A Course in Miracles*

LOFTY DESIRES AND DREAMS

Look at the dreams that you have failed to acknowledge because you fear they are too lofty. What would happen if you stepped out and attempted to reach those dreams? What would your life look like? What skills would you need? What has hindered you from acquiring those skills? Make as many notes as possible of all the reasons your dreams are unrealistic. Your list may include persons, events (wrong school, wrong city), or even history. Make the list as exhaustive as possible.

EXERCISE FOR FORGIVING LOFTY DREAMS

Visualize the person, event, or situation that may have caused you to believe your dreams are too lofty. As best you can look at the reasoning behind the rationalization. For example, I wanted to be a broadcast journalist when I graduated college in 1978. My mother told me that it was very unlikely that I could ever get a position on television as a journalist. I am a dark-skinned female and, at the time, there were perhaps two African-American female reporters in New Orleans, and they all were light skinned.

I managed to get an interview with the producer of one of the television stations because of my perseverance. In hindsight, I truly believe the producer wanted to hire me, but I was way too nervous and insecure to convince him of my ability. Truth is, I was extremely capable, as evidenced by the fact that I was able to secure an interview. He knew before he saw me that I was black. The loftiness of my dream was deterred by my mother's fear of racism, which passed down to me. My insecurities were that I was dark-skinned, and didn't think I was attractive or articulate enough for television. Heck, in hindsight, I could have been Oprah!

So, I needed to forgive my mother, Jim Crow, and heck, even slavery and color-struck mentalities, and accept that that was a part of American history. It's all so funny now, because today I recognize how beautiful, smart and articulate I am and how blessed everyone is to be in my presence The ills of the past have led me to this place, full of more confidence because I now know it was fear that led my mother to believe I couldn't be successful in TV, a fear that was handed down to me.

America wants to see my glow, and what I have to offer, and while that dream may have not been realized I still have all the time I need to realize any and all other dreams. I look at that situation and the young intimidated girl with loving eyes. In looking at her, I re-write the story of her being confident, articulate and engaging.

The producer can't wait to get this young, lovely, dark-skinned woman on his show to showcase her to New Orleans, and let them see the beautiful new talent he has uncovered. She has risen to the top, and is the Oprah of New Orleans, and has gone on to achieve success. What a wonderful new story that has been written!

And then I awaken from the meditation, refreshed, knowing that I can achieve all things. The past is gone, the story has been re-written and there was a totally different outcome. I feel the same exhilaration and excitement I would have felt if I had gotten the job in real life. There is no one I need to be angry with or disappointed in. I got the same feeling of joy I would have experienced if the facts had been different.

This "high" is what I take with me to my new goals and dreams. This vision that lets me know I can achieve all of my goals and no goal is too lofty. Now I can affirm and have the same vibration as a successful Olympic athlete, who is ready for their third gold medal. It's the joy and exhilaration of the success that propels us. We are exceptional beings because we can create that feeling at any time. Oh the joys of imagination, along with the joys of forgiveness. There aren't any culprits in my re-written story; everyone is victorious, everyone is a winner!

Mama is excited because I have broken barriers. The producer is excited because he has brought in a beautiful new talent that New Orleans was lacking before, and now he is the town hero. I am a superstar. I am a successful newscaster in New Orleans with a new talk show. I have gone on to be as successful as Oprah. Yes, it was all in my dreams, but the vibration of success is there, if I simply choose to hold onto it.

It's your dream. You are free to use it as you will, and to keep that vibration buried in your consciousness to use at will. This is how we manifest, this is how we forgive, and this is how we propel ourselves into new achievements.

I have attempted to illustrate through the story of attending a Broadway show how holding onto unforgiveness could cause you to miss the joy of being in the present and missing the beauty of life. Life is a show, and you want to be present for all of it. If you are holding onto the past, then you may miss what is before your eyes in the present.

Our anxiety arises from our worrying about the future. Usually, we are concerned and worried about the future because of a bad experience we had in the past. If we could release the past, then we wouldn't be concerned or stressed out about the future. For example, I may be the type of person who is fearful about being able to pay my bills. Let's say in the past I squandered my money and would come up short when it was time to pay my bills. Because of this, my lights have been cut off or I faced the threat of eviction. So now daily I'm concerned about my bills and I don't get to enjoy my money or the delights that money can offer because I'm too busy fretting about the future.

However, this fretting has not conditioned me enough to save or manage my money. It has only caused me to miss enjoying the present because I'm afraid of tomorrow's bills. I'm sure you can relate to this scenario. Perhaps you aren't in that situation, but I'm sure you know someone who lives like this. If you don't do this to your finances, is there another area in your life where you have had challenges in the past, and now you bring them into your present? So you spend so much time worrying about how things may turn out in the future that you actually end up missing what you may have at your disposal right now.

What are some of the areas where you have been faced with this challenge? Look at them, identify them, and then write out positive affirmations to turn the situation around so that now you can live in the present.

USING AFFIRMATIVE PRAYER:

Let's use as an example the financial predicament of not paying bills on time, and squandering money. I want to release this old pattern of behavior and start a new course of financial responsibility. First things first, I must forgive myself for my past "failures." So my self-talk may go something like this: "I recognize that in the past I have been irresponsible with money. That is the past and is not my present. The past is not the truth of who I am, and I am not held hostage by what may have occurred previously. I am free. Each moment is a new moment, and the only thing that matters is the Holy Instant. And in the Holy Instant I always recognize the truth of who I am, because it is the only thing that is real. I am financially secure and responsible. I pay my bills on time. I release all thoughts of the past, which have held me hostage to late payments, and neglected bills. That is not the truth of who I am."

SPIRITUAL MIND TREATMENT

Now, let's get to your divinity and make this a Spiritual Mind Treatment so that you can scientifically erase the past, and now move forward with a clean slate.

A Spiritual Mind Treatment (SMT) is a technique that was developed by Ernest Holmes, founder of the Science of Mind philosophy. The treatment is an affirming prayer that acknowledges your connection to God, and your Perfection, which is the absolute truth of who you are. Remember how Jesus continuously reminded us of this?

Spiritual Mind Treatments are broken in to 5 steps. This is a scientific method that absolutely works. I have always had faith in prayer, and I have always had amazing results when I believe. What I have found with this type of prayer is that my results come quicker, and I begin to affirm and feel better right away. As Jesus said, it is your belief that makes it so. It is not the prayer; it is your belief that makes it so! SMT is an affirming prayer, which goes to the core of what prayer does. It changes your mind and brings you into the power and presence of the truth of who you are. For more information, please refer to *The Science of Mind* text, by Ernest Holmes.

With SMT, you recognize the truth of your creation and you to speak to the Entity which is All-Powerful and Creative, which is a reflection of your Absolute Truth. You acknowledge Creative Intelligence, Divine Spirit by the name you are most comfortable with. Is it God? Is it Father? Is it Holy Spirit? Is it Jesus? Is it Allah? Is it Jehovah? Is it Source? Is it Mother/Father God? It doesn't matter what name you give it, because God knows you by Spirit.

Since I want to "treat" about my fears around paying bills on time, I need to speak to the attributes of God that relate to Her timeliness and security.

SPIRITUAL MIND TREATMENT (SMT)

Recognition
Acknowledging the truth of My Divine Creator I affirm and state that God is meticulous. God is timely. And God is secure. God has no fears about the past, no anxiety about the future, because God is always in the present.

Unification
I am a divine reflection of My Divine Creator. I was created in the perfect and divine image of my creator, and I am One with Creation.

Realization
Because of the truth of who I am, I declare that I always pay my bills on time. I am always meticulous and in perfect order with my finances. I am secure with my bills and with my finances. I don't hold any fears or regrets about the past, and I live in the present state of timeliness, which means I am anxiety free. I always have more than enough to pay all of my bills.

Thanksgiving
I am grateful for this knowledge. I am grateful for this truth. And I am especially grateful that being made in the

image of my Creator, I am a reflection of all that is good and perfect.

Release

Knowing this to be true, I release and let go. In releasing I realize that there is nothing more that I need to do other than let go and walk in this pure and perfect knowledge of Absolute Truth. And so it is.

The key to praying this affirming prayer is to pray it with knowingness and conviction. You must be convinced of the truth of who YOU are. The key is to acknowledge who your Creator is and the powers that He possesses. You must recognize your unification with this awesome power, recognizing that you are made in the Divine Image of all that is Good. This is what Jesus taught when he said you had these amazing powers. Begin using them daily to transform your life. These amazing wonders are yours simply for the using. Begin today and watch for the amazing results.

Spiritual Mind Treatment is a perfect example of living in the Present. You release all attachment to the past and anxiety about the future. You simply speak your affirmations in the now. I AM. Enough said. No need to focus on yesterday, that has been released. No need to worry about tomorrow, since there is no such thing as tomorrow. Remember the childhood joke, "tomorrow never comes." No truer words have been spoken. With SMT you speak in the NOW, knowing that your truth and your desires are here and present for you.

LIVING IN THE PRESENT

*I have a client, Aretha, who discovered the power
of forgiveness and how the benefits of forgiveness
helped her to live in the present. Her husband
had an issue with exaggerating. He would also
tell lies. The funny thing is that he would lie
about things that he had no reason to lie about. I
believe it was a self-esteem issue; that he exagger-
ated and told out and out lies because he thought
they would make him more impressive to others.*

*Aretha knew Charles had this challenge before
she married him, but she chose to overlook it,
which she later shared with me, bothered her
since the beginning of their romance. As a side
note, most of us, especially women, intuitively
know when a man isn't telling the truth. Men
aren't good liars, and women are adept at seeing
through the façade, even though we may choose
not to challenge our partner on his tall tales.*

*After they were wed, Aretha began challenging
Charles. Now none of his tales were related to
affairs, they were just exaggerations of things like
events and people. For example, Charles would
often exaggerate about places he had visited, ce-
lebrities he knew, or jobs he held. Well, Aretha
was embarrassed by Charles' embellishments and
started challenging him on them. She even called*

him a liar when he lied, and sometimes did so in front of their friends.

Needless to say, this put a huge strain on their marriage. Aretha wanted to forgive and move on, but was afraid such behavior would be tantamount to masking the situation. Aretha asked me for help. How could she forgive this without condoning this behavior that she abhorred? She wanted her husband to stop exaggerating and lying. She loved him but knew that his exaggerations led to frequent arguments that, on the surface, didn't appear to have anything to do with his fabricated stories. They both could admit that it was because he wasn't being truthful, even though Charles would stand behind his stories and swear they were true. Aretha would stand her ground and challenge his lies.

I asked Aretha to look at her own life, to see where she lies or exaggerates. I wanted her to be honest, even if she only did it occasionally, or when she felt it was absolutely necessary. I wanted her to do this in light of the truth that there is no order of difficulty to miracles, and that all are equal. I also wanted her to do this so that it would help her release judgment. In looking at herself, even though she may feel a need to justify the situation, she may have an easier time being empathetic. Also, each situation is an opportuni-

*ty for self-forgiveness. So I didn't want her to pass
up this wonderful opportunity for her to forgive
herself for any and all lies she has told.*

ARETHA'S EXERCISE

To enhance the exercise, I recommended to Aretha that she journal on the latest lie or exaggeration that Charles told and then to journal on the last time she remembered telling a lie or an exaggeration. After she wrote them down, I instructed her to do the following exercise in a meditative state.

1. Hold the journal in your hands, and picture it as one big lie. See the lies meld into one, with no distinction between them.
2. Then enclose the lies with a big bright white light. Imagine this is the Light of God and recognize that Light covers all darkness.
3. See this Light covering the darkness of the lies that she has told as well as the lies that Charles has told. They are all one, no matter when they were told, or how big or little they were. They are all one lie.
4. Light covers darkness. The lies were dark; they are now embraced and enfolded in the light. The lies have disappeared and no longer exist.
5. Now it is time for reflection on the TRUTH, and that the TRUTH always comes forth from your mouth and from Charles' mouth.

This is not a denial. Aretha is now ready to let the past go, and to now embrace the present as the Holy Instant. The Holy Instant is where truth resides. The past is an illusion! Remember, we cannot get it back, we can't hold it, we can't see it, we can only replay it in our mind.

It is now time for Aretha to make affirmations, and to do an affirming prayer, such as a Spiritual Mind Treatment. Because Aretha was able to look at herself, she was then able to invite Charles into her prayer. Even her approach to Charles reflected this as she shared with him that she wanted to change her behaviors and she thought it would be helpful to him as well as her. This is a true benefit to self-reflection, we see ourselves as we look at others.

Charles was willing and able to participate in the treatment because, I believe, he felt the sincerity in Aretha's approach. Forgiveness recognizes that we all have the potential to "miss the mark," but when we open our eyes to the truth of who we are, all is well. All is in Divine Order and all is PERFECT and complete. Aretha was blessed to have Charles participate in the prayer with her. I believe it would have been just as effective even if Charles chose not to participate.

Forgiveness Allows You to be Accountable

Self-Forgiveness simply means I am able be accountable for my life. Since I don't harbor any guilt about what I have manifested in my life, I am able to accept that I created it, and take responsibility for changing it. I'M GUILT FREE!
~ This Is Bliss

What if I told you that you personally created all your illnesses; that every discord in your life, you were the one who created them? This could range from a cheating lover, to disrespectful children to illness. They all came about because of you! If you are like most people who hear or read this, you are probably shouting "no way!" Circumstances and situations caused them, you likely believe. If you do accept this proposition as correct, then you may also decide that it is true because you are a bad person. I mean, what sort of person would cause himself or herself to be ill? It would have to be someone who didn't love herself or himself very much, right? And if that were so, then you would also end up feeling pretty guilty about doing this to yourself, wouldn't you?

Most people don't accept the Truth that we create all the situations in our lives because to do so would cause them unbearable anxiety. If this were the case, without self-forgiveness, we would all be on anti-depressants! I believe we create even so called "natural disasters." That is a hard pill to swallow if you are unwilling to accept the truth about forgiveness. Since there are "no idle thoughts, and we are always creating," then that means we entertain some pretty bad thoughts, which ultimately create all the madness and sadness that occur in our lives.

Chances are, if you are reading this book you have heard about The Law of Attraction. This Universal Law does not discriminate. Consequently, whatever we focus on and think about are attracted into our lives. So if this is correct, and there are numerous scientific studies that support the accuracy of this Law, then you want to change your thinking in order to attract your deepest heart's desires.

Sometimes it is hard for us to reverse the process because we can get caught up in what we *may* have created. As a Bliss Coach, I get to help my clients understand that there should not be any guilt associated with what you have created. If there is, then it is difficult to rectify the situation and turn it around. Simply put, we are all creators. We create with our thoughts and with our words. Remember, in the beginning was the Word! The paper/computer that you are reading these words on were created from a thought. Words were spoken to develop these creations. This is true even on a metaphysical level.

Now, let's look at how a step-by-step approach may aid or hinder us in our healing and ability to manifest the life we desire.

- As a creator, I get to create the kind of life I desire.
- If I am creating my life, and bad things are happening to me, then I must be doing something wrong.
- If I'm doing something wrong, then I must feel guilty.
- If I am feeling guilty, then I create the cycle all over again to manifest more bad things in my life.
- To stop feeling guilty and to correct what I'm doing wrong I need to be able to look at my life guilt free.
- In order to look at my life guilt free, I must be able to forgive myself.
- When I am able to look at what is going on in my life "guilt free," I am in a better position to change it if I desire.

FORGIVENESS EXERCISE:
BEING ACCOUNTABLE

Please make sure you are in a meditative state when you do this exercise. You may choose to wear white, light a candle and put on some soft, New Age music, or any meditation music that will allow your chakras to open. Begin this exercise with a prayer of intent. Let Spirit/Source/God/Mother/Father God know that it is your desire to remove all blocks to unforgiveness, to help you live a more blissful life. Invite the angels to join in on the session with you, to support you to opening your heart and mind to complete this exercise.

Choose an area in your life that you would like to change.

_____

_____

_____

_____

_____

_____

_____

_____

_____

_____

Now, using the Law of Attraction as your guide, how might you be attracting this into your life? Write your thoughts without thinking about what you are writing. Use the space below or write in your personal journal. Let your pen flow, and allow your intuition to point the way. If it is an illness, you may want to refer to a metaphysical guide, such as Louise Hay's, *You Can Heal Your Life.*

Forgiveness Hastens the Manifestation Process

The better I feel, the more in tune I am with the true desires of my heart. The more in tune I am with the desires of my heart, the better I position myself to make the Law of Attraction work in my favor.
~ This Is Bliss

We are all creators! We were created in the image of the Magnificent Creator, which means He gave us the attributes of a creator. If you don't believe you are a creator, look at your life and how it has unfolded. The job you had, you created it by your thoughts and your actions. Someone created this medium, and, of course, I created this book.

First it was a thought then I used WORDs to create. This is true in every aspect of our life. There is a LAW of Creation, just as there are Universal Laws that govern every aspect of our life. The question is, what is it you that want to create?

The Higher our vibration, that is, the better we feel, the more in tuned we are to what we are creating. This means that our ability to create the things our heart desires is increased. Since forgiveness lead to better feelings, this means we are able to create more of what we truly desire.

If you are holding grudges or nursing fears because of judgment, then you are hindering the manifestation of your true heart's desires. Look around you and examine your life. Now answer the question, what is showing up in your life that you would like less of or have leave altogether? What are some of the hindrances that may be keeping you from being happy? Do you think it is someone else, or something else? Make a note of what is appearing in your life that you do not like, thing that make you sad. What is it that blocks your joy? Is it a job you don't like? Is it a relationship gone sour? Is it not being in a relationship at all? Is it a physical illness, or do you dislike your physical appearance? Is it a lack of money? Now note all the reasons that you think these things are showing up in your life. If you can specifically relate it to a person, please do so. If you think it is history, or some unavoidable circumstance, please indicate it. Write down whatever comes to mind without thinking too much about it.

THINGS IN MY LIFE I DON'T LIKE or WANT:

_____

_____

_____

_____

_____

_____

_____

_____

_____

_____

_____

_____

_____

_____

_____

_____

_____

_____

_____

_____

_____

_____

_____

WHO or WHAT has caused these situations to appear in your life? Begin journaling and blaming circumstances, events, other people, and yourself. Allow the pen to flow, without reservation and judgment.

_____
_____
_____
_____
_____
_____
_____
_____
_____
_____
_____
_____
_____
_____
_____
_____
_____
_____
_____
_____
_____
_____
_____
_____
_____

Now go back to your Bliss scale and remind yourself how you want to reach a Bliss Level of ten or greater! Once you have reminded yourself, and have had an appropriate talk with yourself about how important it is for you to lead a joyful, happy life, you are ready to reach out and forgive each one of these people, situations and events.

FORGIVENESS EXERCISE: LETTER WRITING

Please make sure you are in a meditative state when you do this exercise. You may choose to wear white light a candle and put on some soft, New Age music, or any meditation music, which will allow your chakras to open. Begin this exercise with a prayer of intent. Let Spirit/Source/God/Mother/Father God know that it is your desire to remove all blocks to unforgiveness that keep you from living a blissful life. Invite the angels to support join in on the session with you, to support you in opening your heart and mind.

Now it is time for you to write a forgiving love letter to each situation. Let the situation know how much it disappointed you, how hurtful it was, and how you ache because of it. Pour out your heart to the situation and explain how let down you feel.

After you have poured your heart out, and expressed all the wrongdoing and the pain you feel, it is time for you to look for the good in the situation. Ask Spirit to work with you and help you see it. Spirit is always delighted to help you see the good in any situation. Ask the Holy Spirit and your Angels to guide you and allow you to find any possible good in this situation. Even allow the situation or person's Higher Self to speak directly to you. Allow your pen to glide across the paper as the thoughts come to you. Perhaps the thought or situation wants to speak to you directly and call you by name. The situation may write a letter to you directly.

As you reflect and journal, you may begin to see goodness because what has happened is allowing you to feel pain, and in experiencing pain you are better able to understand the contrast of pain and joy. The point is to leave no stone unturned in what good could possibly come out of the situation.

Once you have felt the goodness that could come from the situation it is now time to allow the gratitude to well up in your heart. You are now ready to forgive. Allow the situation or person to know that you have forgiven it, that you are releasing it from bondage. As you release the situation, let them know that in releasing them, you are also releasing yourself, because you know your pain has been tied to them. You let them go, and you free them. Talk to them as you would talk to a four year old who is totally disappointed because she fell down while trying to learn to ride her bike. She is now afraid, and you are letting her know all is well. That everything will be okay. Open your heart to total forgiveness, letting the person know sincerely that it really is okay. There are no degrees to "sin" and you forgive it as easily as you forgive a scraped knee.

Now be in total gratitude. Thank the person or event for being in your life and allowing you to grow. Now that you are healing you feel so much better and the good feeling is just what you desired. Let them know how much better you feel. How much lighter you feel. Feel the weight taken off of you and invite in good feelings to replace any prior bad feelings you had. Experience the lightness and joy that are entering your heart. The angels have assisted you in this exercise and they are delighted to help you release the judgment. Thank everyone involved, and feel your lips curl towards a smile, and perhaps even laughter, as you write the letter.

Do this as often as necessary with every situation, and feel your body and emotions as your heart releases judgment to everything and everyone. Your heart is lighter. You feel lighter and happier. As you feel this lightness and JOY entering your heart and life, now is the perfect time to make your desires known.

Start speaking your desires aloud, affirming their presence in your life NOW. Your vibration is raising and the Universe feels your Joy and goodness and is definitely ready to support you in having all of your desires. Now you can MAKE your dreams come true!

AFFIRMATIONS

A quick word on affirmations: Affirmations are an excellent way to manifest your heart's desires. The key to making affirmations work is to speak them in the present as if what you desire already exist. It is much more powerful to say "I am a magnet for money, money flows to me easily and effortlessly," than to say, "I will make more money. I will get a job making more money." Time is to be used to your benefit. When you speak affirmations in the now, you are affirming your belief that your desires are already done!

Forgiveness is Healing

To heal is to make happy. Think how many opportu-
nities you have to gladden yourselves, and how many
you have refused. This is exactly the same as telling
you that you have refused to heal yourselves.
~ *A Course in Miracles*

There is now indisputable evidence that many illnesses are self-inflicted through anger, remorse, sadness,
unreleased toxic emotions and many other negative states.
All of these emotional states arise from unforgiveness! We
must look upon every situation that cause these states and
release them through the practice of forgiveness. It is critical to our healing process and our overall state of physical
and emotional well-being.

There are often times when we may not be able to
pinpoint exactly what has triggered an unhealthy reaction.

Often, when we do pinpoint it, we may not recognize it as an opportunity to forgive. For instance, Louise Hay in her book, *You Can Heal Your Life,* states that bad breath comes from anger and revenge thoughts. Anger and revenge thoughts speak to a need to forgive, release and let go. Hay's book also says knee problems suggest a stubborn ego and pride along with an inability to bend and be flexible. Can you see how that can be traced back to a need to be right, which is associated with judgment? Also, there may be a place for self-forgiveness in your inflexibility.

A very dear friend, Preston Edwards, wrote a book on laughing his way to health. In his book, *You Have Cancer,* he talks about how he made a concerted effort to laugh and be happy. His joy, not surprisingly, led to his healing. As the above quote from ACIM states, when you are happy you are healing. If you are holding a grudge, if you are in judgment, if you are feeling any remorse, or anger, then you are experiencing moments of joylessness. This is an indication that you have an opportunity to forgive.

Anytime you are feeling joyless, or feeling hopeless, and not laughing very much, is the time to look within and see who, where, or what you may need to forgive. When you are faced with any illness, this is also the time to "forgive those who have trespassed against us." This is an excellent way to begin your healing process and better yet, a great way to eliminate many illnesses.

Only my condemnation injures me.
Only my own forgiveness sets me free.
~ A Course in Miracles

Do not forget today that there can be no form of suffering that fails to hide an unforgiving thought. Nor can there be a form of pain forgiveness cannot heal.
- A Course in Miracles

As you consciously practice forgiveness, you may notice that aches and pains begin to diminish. And as they reoccur in your life, look at them as an opportunity to forgive. Search to see what it is that you are holding onto, that has bound you physically.

Daily meditations and Spiritual Mind Treatments are excellent remedies for all forms of sickness. As a Reiki practitioner, I also call on the healing power of my clients' angels to help guide the beautiful Life Force Energy that is available to aid in their healing. Your angels are always eager to help. Please use their assistance as well.

Forgiveness Enhances Relationships

In the holy instant it is understood that the past is gone, and with its passing the drive for vengeance has been uprooted and has disappeared. The stillness and the peace of now enfold you in perfect gentleness. Everything is gone except the truth.
~ A Course in Miracles

It would appear to be a logical conclusion that once you release the past, then your relationships are enhanced. You are no longer holding onto the past, and you are much freer to enjoy your life, your love, and experience bliss. Think about it, what are you angry about? What has been the cause of strife in your relationships? Now what would happen if you released it to the oblivion of the past, and never looked at it again? Are you afraid that if you forgive it, that it will repeat itself? Well, I believe that if you don't forgive it, it is bound to haunt you. Either in repeating itself in your current relationship, or preventing you from enjoying new relationships, or worse yet, preventing you from engaging in any relationships!

I have been married and divorced twice. Well, actually, the second one doesn't count because I was able to get it annulled. And even though I wasn't married to my oldest daughter's father, as many of you can attest, the discord that a "baby daddy" can bring can equal marital strife.

I am grateful that it was never my intent to paint a bad picture in my daughter's head about her father. To this day she cannot say she has heard me say one bad thing about her father. And I made sure they had a relationship. I was blessed to recognize that her father is a part of whom she is, and if I disparaged him, well what was I saying about her? After all, she is half of him. Besides, what in the world would I be saying about myself? After all, I chose to be with him.

Again, I like myself too much to intentionally make myself feel poorly. The moment I hold my partner in contempt, then in essence I am holding myself in contempt. I am saying and reinforcing how "stupid" I am for bad judgment. I am saying I am not worthy of good relationships. Now, neither of these statements is true. To many, it may appear that I am in denial because I don't go around bad mouthing my past partners. I don't think it's a denial, I think it's a matter of what I choose to focus on, and how I choose to see the world.

I believe this approach to relationships is another benefit of forgiveness. It recognizing my connection to others,

I am less likely to point fingers because I know it is a reflection of me. And although I may not be "perfect" in this illusionary world, I choose to focus on my Divinity. It doesn't mean I don't grow in my experience; it just means I am more focused on enjoying life and living blissfully. My mantra is, "don't believe the hype," that you must live in your shortcomings. I have a friend who loves to say, "I'm a work in progress." I believe this is a cop out, a way of denying your truth. I believe God created us whole and perfect, and when I begin talking about being a "work in progress," then what I am doing is living in the past, not the present.

The truth of who I am resides in this Holy Instant. And what is true for me is also true for you. So in my relationships, I choose to live in the present. Now what happens to the hurts and the pains and the issues that are occurring in our relationships? How do I walk away from something that isn't serving me well, and that I am ready to leave?

The answer is *I just do it!* Yes, I walk away if that is what I truly feel led to do. I try my best to make it work, but when it is time to leave, I leave. I leave recognizing that the person I have related to, that I have had my issues with, is a reflection of me. What we were going through was not working for us. But that doesn't mean my ex is bad, no more than I am. When I subscribe to "there is no order of difficulty to miracles," then I am also subscribing to the truth that my partner is no guiltier then I am.

In my marriage, my spouse had a hard time holding down a job because he was an alcoholic. I am not an alcoholic, and it's rare that I have more than one drink. However, I have other excesses. One is I love to eat. I can also be an excessive talker. So what makes me so different? My spouse had a difficult time holding down a job. I have challenges with being on time. What makes me better? I decided to end the marriage, but I sure can see a lot of good in this man. For one, he was able to attract me, so that makes him a great attracter. He was very neat and always smelled good. He was the perfect lover for me. The list could go on and on, so when I reflect on the relationship I see him in a good light. That's because I know I am always reflecting myself!

I believe once you begin practicing forgiveness, you develop a "play and stay" attitude. You become more adept at working through problems and situations. Your patience also grows. In practicing forgiveness you have also enhanced your ability to manifest, so you are able to better create the type of relationship that you want.

As you forgive yourself, you are forgiving your past choices, and you are better able to break the pattern or cords that tie you to these poor choices. So your relationship choices begin to change drastically. You will find that people irritate you less, and the people who you thought you had problems with will either disappear or problems you had with them will dissipate. Forgiveness changes you, changes your vibration and changes those around you. Your perception of life and others has changed as well. As a result of all these changes, you have raised your Bliss Level!

Affirmations are a powerful tool for enhancing and improving your relationships. Please use these in conjunction with forgiveness, with your meditations and Spiritual Mind Treatment to attract the right people in your life and to improve your present relationships. I have successfully used affirmations to manifest many powerful changes in my life, and I am blessed with a beautiful relationship which I believe came as a result of the following affirmation. I wrote this affirmation 50 times in my best handwriting. It was my intention to write it 100 times. My partner, who I attracted, says his intention and desire for me covered the other 50 that I didn't write.

> *"I am in a joyful intimate relationship*
> *with someone who truly loves me."*

Choose the affirmation that works for you. Please be sure to say it as "I am," not "I will," or "I want." Remember to say it as knowing that exactly what you say will happen!

Giving and Receiving Love

One thought, completely unified, will serve to unify all thought. This is the same as saying one correction will suffice for all correction, or that to forgive one brother wholly is enough to bring salvation to all minds.

To learn that giving and receiving are the same has special usefulness, because it can be tried so easily and seen as true.
~ A Course in Miracles

One of the lessons that *A Course in Miracles* stresses is that giving and receiving, just like teaching and learning, are one and the same. You are unable to give what you do not have, and in giving you are turning up your vibration to be more, and to have more of the same. This is a Universal Law, and its application works in both the positive and the negative. What we must remember with Universal Laws is that they always work—whether what we get is positive or negative, they always work.

My brother had a really difficult time making the transition from a small town in California to Baltimore city. He made the trip because his marriage had fallen apart, and he was distraught over the break up. He has seven beautiful children; still there was absolutely no reconciliation between he and his wife. I invited him here to help him overcome feelings of isolation and depression.

When he arrived, his anger about his marriage permeated his conversations. Of course, he often saw his image reflected back to him in all sorts of situations. One day he said, "All the bus drivers here are rude!" He said he'd never encountered such rude people. He said he would be at the bus stop and the bus driver would drive right by him. Or he'd be running for the bus, would be virtually at the door, and the driver would keep right on going. If he asked for directions, they were rude. Overall, Baltimore bus drivers were just plain mean and grumpy people. It didn't matter the driver's gender; all of them were rude. He couldn't believe Baltimore would tolerate such nastiness in its public servants.

I suggested that he try a simple experiment. I encouraged him to go out intending to meet very nice and cordial bus drivers. He was to extend this thought to everyone that he met on the bus. He would need, I continued, to practice smiling and to genuinely feel in his heart that everyone was glad to see him and happy to help.

To my surprise, he took me up on the challenge. He practiced the exercise to the best of his ability for two to three days. And lo and behold, without me even reminding him or asking him, he came back to me excited that the experiment worked. He said he was meeting the nicest bus drivers! They stopped for him, they greeted him, and the passengers on the bus all seemed to take on a nicer persona!

This was a prime example of giving and receiving being the same. The simple act of changing his mind, and his mood, changed his entire world. What if we did this every day? What if upon awakening you expected to have a good day? What if you expected everyone to be happy to see you and would treat you that way? Do you think your energy would reflect that expectation, because you were in a giving and receiving mood? It works, and if you don't believe me, try this simple exercise that I have done from time to time with amazing results.

FORGIVENESS EXERCISE: HOLY ENCOUNTER!

Pretend for a full day that everyone you see is someone you hold near and dear to your heart. It should be someone that sets your soul on fire. You want to pretend that you have not seen this person in a very long time, and you are greeting them for the first time in a long time as they just stepped off the plane. You will now use the image of the person who represents extreme joy for you. Throughout the day, everyone you see should receive the same vibration and smile that you would feel in greeting your special person.

For me, it was the image of my son stepping off the plane from college. The thought of seeing him after being away a full semester would light up my life, as I imagined seeing him come through the corridor after getting off the plane. My son has a smile that absolutely lights up the world when he is happy to see someone. And of course, that smile can't help but be reflected back to him.

Yes, I kept a smile plastered on my face, and my very being inside was extremely happy. And boy, I received that same vibration back! There were moments when I would forget and go back to my usual feelings; however, as soon as I remembered I would continue with the experiment. It turned out to be one of the most joyful days I had ever lived!

Whenever I find that I am encountering grumpy people or poor service, all I need to do is check within to see how I am feeling on the inside. Once I do the internal check, and turn my vibration up on the inside, I notice that everyone around me attitude becomes more positive.

As an additional benefit to this experiment, you may also pretend that everyone is a loved one whom you adore and cherish, and whom you want to have a really good day. With this element added to the experience, if you encounter someone who appears to be having a tough day and are not reflecting the vibration that you are sharing, then you treat them with the same compassion you would a loved one.

I have found moments of just allowing them to be, which means holding a space in my heart to allow them to feel bad, opens a path which helps them turn around. I remember one of the days when I was very consciously aware of practicing this exercise that I encountered a sour store clerk. I held a space in my heart for her, and I could tell she needed to feel some love. So I asked her very gently if she was okay. She shared that she was having a hard time that day, and was considering quitting because she was very unhappy in her position. I expressed compassion and told her I was sorry she was feeling bad. (Isn't this the same thing you would do for a loved one.) She told me thank you, and that she needed to hear that from someone. I could see her countenance change from that conversation. She was no longer sour towards me, and as I watched her service the customers after me, I saw she no longer had that grumpy attitude. Of course, this exchange made me feel better too!

This change in our attitude, and our perception, as well as the way we greet our neighbor, is our way of "saving the world" and being the "light of the world." That is not a small feat! This is major as we change one attitude at a time, we get to experience bliss and share bliss. Why do you think Jesus said the second commandment was just as important as the first? "To love thy neighbor as thyself," is a commandment which all the prophets and upon which all the laws are based. Our love for self, and our love for our neighbor, is our healing to the world!

GRACE FORGIVES HER FATHER

After forgiving her father for abandoning her, Grace was able to experience the joy of having her father in her life. At the same time, his life was also turned around. She writes:

> *Father's Day is the time we celebrate our fathers.*
> *Yet for most of my life, fatherhood has been an*
> *enigma. It was something I studied, read and*

learned about through movies, church, and other families. It was not, unfortunately, something I was personally familiar with because my father was absent during my childhood. This has made defining myself very difficult. I've even walked Hallmark store aisles in search of cards for a father I barely knew.

Almost three years ago, I had a defining moment: Hurricane Katrina. My absent father was among its survivors. In the blink of an eye, hundreds of questions ran through my mind: Why should I help manage the recovery of a dislocated father who abandoned me? Why should I facilitate the nurturing to self-sufficiency of someone who didn't nurture me? Why should I suspend my life to manage his personal affairs? How could he leave me with a broken male image? And most significantly, where was he when I needed him?

Ultimately, only one question would be answered in order for me to make the decision from which time would forever be changed: "Would I live up to the name my birth father gave me, Grace, which means to emanate mercy and compassion. True grace calls for us to be selfless and bless unconditionally, regardless of the past. I had been wounded, was still wounded, by the first man who was to love me, cherish me, and tell me that I'm all that. His absence set me up for a string of broken hearts and unhealthy male relationships. And yet,

I was willing to open my heart to finally shed light on those wounds, and hopefully heal them.

Today, I'm proud to say my father stands again on his own, recovered, financially stable and self-sufficient. I am also proud to tell you that we have established a healthier relationship, one that continues to evolve as he takes a more active role in my life. He sends me emails, writes me poems, and even shares his favorite country songs with me. We are communicating openly, honestly and frequently. This healing has been nothing short of a glimpse of God's wonder. I learned that forgiveness heals the heart and unconditional love heals the soul. That little girl who lacked the foundation that only a father can provide is now stable and grounded. I am supported, loved, special, cherished and whole. I now carry into every male encounter this aura of grace.

Asking for Forgiveness

*The Platinum Rule: Do unto others
as they would have done unto them.*
~ This Is Bliss

*Do you prefer that you be right or happy? Be
you glad that you are told where happiness
abides, and seek no longer elsewhere.*
~ A Course in Miracles

*The beautiful relationship you have with all your brothers
is a part of you because it is a part of God Himself.*
~ A Course in Miracles

*O Divine Master, grant that I may not so
much seek to be consoled, as to console.*
~ Prayer of Saint Francis

My beloved, we have talked about forgiving others, and forgiving ourselves, which essentially is the same as forgiving others. Now it is time for us to discuss the importance of seeking forgiveness.

I must admit that as I undertook this journey of forgiveness, I practically focused entirely on my need to forgive others. I also recognized early on that in forgiving others, I was also forgiving myself. It simply comes down to the truth that giving and receiving are one and the same. This truth is also rooted in the recognition that my brother and I are one.

As I practiced these spiritual principles, I started recognizing that everything is colored by my perception. As soon as I changed my mind about someone, or about some thing, then I had a new perspective and things changed. I was able to create magic. But here I was recognizing this difference. What about those whom I offended? Those who, during those moments I had forgotten MY divinity, and consequently forgot to recognize THEIR divinity? What about them?

There were and are many opportunities in my relationships for me to come to this awareness. So when I change my perception of the situation, does that mean everyone around me has immediately changed. Well, it could happen, but more often than not it doesn't automatically happen. Yes, there are many moments and opportunities for us to seek forgiveness.

I have a horrible relationship with a sister-in-law. There are very few people that I have this type of relationship with, but she is my Achilles heel. I continue to work on healing this relationship within myself, so that that healing might radiate out to her. But the only way for true healing to occur is for me to reach out to her. I will always be bound by this, unless I do so. And I need to do this from the perspective of, "would I rather be happy or right?" As long as I continue to hold her in judgment, I am also binding myself. Even though there is a part of me that believes I have righteous and earned indignation.

I took this sister-in-law in and six of her children because she was having difficulty managing alone in California. I got my brother here and he was still struggling, but he no longer lived with me. I am blessed with a huge home, and am the type of person who easily opens her home to everyone. So I welcomed her here, along with her children. I even sent bus fare for them to travel here.

She stayed with me for more than one and a half years. I found her children to be rather rude. They didn't understand the common courtesy of saying "Good Morning," and no matter how I tried I couldn't get it out of them. Seeing that they couldn't comply with that simple request, I imagined that there were other underlying issues. Unfortunately, I didn't tell my sister-in-law how long she could stay or what her financial obligations were. After she'd been in my home for more than a year rent free, I asked her to start paying, since she had found a job. That's when things started to breakdown. Nasty words were exchanged. I felt used and betrayed because of the things my brother told me she said about my daughter and me. I had chosen to be offended. I had lied to myself, claiming I wanted nothing in return; consequently, I didn't know how to articulate my true desires and needs.

I also came to believe that her children's rudeness stemmed from a resentment that she harbored towards me, and shared with them behind closed doors. After all, in my view, I was constantly giving. My daughter and I bought back-to-school clothes for the kids, and made sure they were set with Christmas gifts.

I got obnoxious and fed up. I told her she had to move immediately. I wasn't prepared for any discussion. I was just ready for her to leave. I felt she had invaded my space enough, and I wasn't getting anything in return. I placed a financial amount on it, but it really had nothing to do with money. It had everything to do with me feeling violated and unappreciated. I wanted more from her. But I never considered that maybe she couldn't give more, and more importantly, that she was a reflection of me! Perhaps it was also cultural—she is from Malaysia—or some other pain that I was not aware of. It really didn't matter, because it was still a reflection of me. The more I suppressed and refused to acknowledge my needs, the more apparent it was that she wasn't fulfilling my needs in return for what I felt I was giving her.

So who is right and who is wrong? Does it even matter? The question is, do I want to heal this situation or do I want it to forever haunt me. As I stated, she is one of the few people in the world with whom I have this animosity. It's a decision I need to make to heal this wound. I remember my grandmother telling an aunt, who was bitterly angry and unforgiving with someone that she can never get to heaven with that person on her wings! Here's the bottom line, no matter what, my occasional negative thoughts of my sister-in-law are weighing down my wings. These thoughts are lowering my Bliss Level, and keeping me from feeling the Kingdom within.

Moreover, this enmity is also invading my sister-in-law healing process, especially if she is not intentionally practicing forgiveness towards those who have "offended" her. So, in extending an apology, or seeking forgiveness from her, I have aided in my healing *and* in hers! By verbally extending an apology to her, I am making myself feel better because I am able to release and let go. With the verbal healing I am saying, *I would rather be at peace than "right."* With my verbal apology to her, I am extending that same peace to her.

It doesn't matter who is right and who is wrong. It doesn't matter whether I have all the details correct or not. My memory is bad. Perhaps I did some horrific things unknowingly, and perhaps she didn't say or harbor the horrific things towards me that I thought she did. But I must release this and let it go, so that I may know true joy.

As of the writing of this chapter, I have not yet made that move. I have decided to do it in a letter and a phone call. The pain between us has been going on for years. But I want the cord to be cut. I want it to end, and I want to be free. I also want her to be free.

In apologizing, I know it doesn't make sense for me to try to explain why I did what I did. When someone steps on your toe, you want to hear, "I'm sorry." Not that your foot was in the way, or "I didn't see your foot there." What you really want to hear is a real sincere, "I am sorry." A sorry which says, "I feel the pain that I have caused you, and I am sorry." A sorry that says, "If I had it to do all over again, I wouldn't hurt you." A sorry, which in no way holds THEM accountable but comes from your heart, that you take FULL responsibility for. That's the kind of "I'm sorry" that heals.

This is the kind of apology that I will extend to my sister-in-law. An apology that says, "I forgot to see you as the Perfect Divine Child of God that you are. I didn't do my part in recognizing we are one! Now I do, and for that I am truly sorry." Please recognize that those aren't the words I will use with her, because she is not on this same forgiveness path that I am on, and those words would not be appropriate for her.

My Letter,

> *Dear Lina,*
>
> *I am truly sorry for the things I have done to offend you while you stayed in my home. You and your children were a blessing to me in more ways than one, and I am grateful that you are in our family. I am sincerely sorry for speaking mean words to you and for betraying any trust you may have placed in me. I can only imagine how that must have made you feel.*
>
> *Please accept my sincerest apologies, and know that if I had it to do all over again I would do things differently.*
>
> *May God's joy, peace and blessings be with you and your family forever and ever!*
>
> *Love always,*
> *Patsy*

FORGIVENESS EXERCISE: UNCOVERING WHO OR WHAT TO FORGIVE

Please make sure you are in a meditative state when you do this exercise. You may choose to wear white, light a candle and put on some soft New Age music, or any meditation music that will allow your chakras to open. Begin this exercise with a prayer of intent. Let Spirit/Source/God/Mother Father God know that it is your desire to remove all blocks to unforgiveness so that you might live a more Blissful Life. Invite the angels to join in on the session with you, to help you open your heart and mind to complete this exercise.

Step 1

Once you are in a relaxed and meditative state, ask Spirit to help you identify anyone who may hold a grievance or grudge against you. Write down their name(s). It may be someone from first grade, or the clerk who assisted you yesterday, just allow Spirit to let the names and situations flow freely across the paper.

Step 2

Now that you have identified whom or what you need to forgive, place your hand on the paper and call out the person's name, or state the situation. Ask them to become present in your heart and in your mind. Ask them to please forgive you, and to feel your love. Allow them to see the Light of God in you as you see the Light of God in them. Allow your spirits to heal and touch and even to embrace in a hug. Feel the love wash over the two of you as the awareness of the presence of love heals the situation.

Step 3

Allow your Higher Self to direct you in any additional forgiveness exercise that you may need to perform. Spirit will direct you to reach out to the person individually, if that is required. Sometimes, that is not feasible, and the above exercise will be sufficient. Trust the feeling that comes over you. You will know the feeling is from God if it comes in peace and not out of guilt. You will know deep down inside the exercise that needs to be taken. Be sure to thank God for the healing work that has been done!

Afterword

Today I let Christ's vision look upon all things for me and judge them not, but give each one a miracle of love instead.
~ *A Course in Miracles*

I simply chose to see things differently.
~ *This is Bliss*

If you are ready, and have begun to incorporate these tools and principles into your life, then you are ready to see magic happen and watch the miracles unfold. The *miracle* actually begins to unfold before your very eyes as you watch your "brother" transform. The transformation is simply your perception. Your acknowledgement that the only thing real is LOVE, and that you are made of 100% Love, and what is true for you is true for your brother!

You are at peace, you no longer hold grudges! You have forgiven yourself, you have forgiven your neighbor, you have even forgiven God. So what is there to be angry about? Nothing, right? Because NOW you are living in the present!! When moments of insanity occur and you think otherwise, you know the steps to take to correct it. You recognize that you are the only one truly accountable for your happiness, and you have discovered that *your* happiness is a gift to others!

The miracle and magic is happening simply because we choose to see differently. You have discovered that seeing through rose-colored glasses is like having the "vision of Christ."

I'm seeing you with the eyes of Christ, the vision of God. I'm sending you Love, Light and Laughter and I know your journey will be a Blissful one. Bliss: The ecstatic joy of heaven, perfect serene happiness. This is our true state, and this is our life.

Blissfully yours,
PJ Cannon

Forgiveness is Bliss

Patsy (Age 34)

Kami, Patsy (age 56) and Mikeela

Walk you in glory, with your head held high,
and fear no evil. ~ A Course in Miracles

CPSIA information can be obtained at www.ICGtesting.com
Printed in the USA
BVOW071623150712

295205BV00001B/1/P